Between Our Eyes That Fall

shihori obata

Table of Contents

***

Between Our Eyes That Fall

I Still Don't Know
What Touches Them

There's a feeling that's not mine –
But this is where I live.

To a Far Away
You

There are eyes that crave the living – And I say words not meant for me just hoping that they can still hear my whispers. Maybe because I know. Black ink gets rubbed into empty spaces and it smears. There are distortions in quiet places and remnants of quiet souls everywhere.

Even If For Just
One Moment

There were times when the sky turned white.
And stars appeared beneath my feet
And my fingertips were painted with galaxies.
I think my eyes grew kinder then –
Lost – of time and past.
Having forgotten the shape of the universe –

My Eyes Become the Sky

Happiness is a pale emotion. It is a wash of white in photography. They're in small smiles and the giggles behind inside-jokes. They're in long walks and cold coffee in hand and cool winds and friends. They're in skies – deep blue – looking down into our own. Into endlessness –

I hope.

A Confession

I don't want these words I say – to mean words. I want these words to fall apart and begin to be nothing. I want to speak in a language of both truths and lies in one. I want the spectrum of what is there and I want to be okay – saying everything that is nonsense. I want my presence to mean everything that couldn't possibly be there – and There – bares the ghost that says "I can't. I can't. I can't."

When Was the Last Time?

I lost sight of you –
When there was fear.
And I'd take strolls alone at midnight
And lay on park benches with tears –
I couldn't stop
Nor understand – Reflections of night
Skies within me – And I'd stay searching
For stars – There –
Until I disappeared
Me and my Fear.

Just Another
Story

I came across the mirage of you once. Walking. Absent-mindedly alive – the image of you vague like fish below ice. Faded and gone because you live somewhere else than here and I felt so envious – Yearning for grays and hazy vapors because I could no longer feel the colors of this place, here.

The heart can see too. And I think that is where much of fear comes from. Because when the eyes can't see – and then the heart can't see – Well, will you then disappear forever from me?

In Another Life

It's a bad thing
To not feel – Anything.
And I couldn't force myself to feel things I didn't feel.
So I lied –
To myself.
And I told myself a different story
And thought in words of poetry.

Because otherwise – I can't feel.
And what kind of person would I be then?

Thoughts that Come
To Walk With Me

You were so engrossed, so bewildered
Not in the scene around you
But in the ground
Passing by – beneath you

Past and Present

Do you remember the past – when the snow came down fast and the world was cold and our eyes blinded white from start to end – I can't remember anything after that but – in this moment, you are warm. And I remember and see the past and this memory, and your warmth keeps everything else that killed me slowly away.

It keeps
all of that
Away.

Black and White

It is so hard. To relay to others the truth of myself when all I can see of me is a fabricated mess. I've been shredded apart and I walk this world in tatters and mismatched patches to hold the rest of me together.

What am I to show them?

The feeling I feel most –

This?

shihori obata

Everything is Nothing
But Love

Reminder
To Self

When rejection hurts you and it stings you this late into the night –
don't sleep. Do something. Relive in your own moments of strength
and self-conviction and find yourself again – Then go to sleep
Forgive – Then sleep. And know that you are able and whole just as
much then as from this moment forth.

Today – much like yesterday –
I still do not know
That you've died.

Blue

I oftentimes lose the feeling of love from constantly going under.
And constantly staying under. I guess during those times, there is no
room in me or near me to feel love. And so, I lose the ability to feel it
– And I forget what it was once like to feel it. But – once in a while,
something pulls me back up. And – I felt that today. And I still felt...
at a loss. I looked up and it was like staring at the strangeness of a
beautiful sky and feeling once again what it was like to be beneath it.
But – along with that feeling came another – of distance. I need to
live. I need to keep myself from drowning in my own sea – within me.

Pink

Distant lights dance across stars and streams. And I have eyes that
swim in forest shadows. If only you could see these things that live
in me –

Live too – As much –
In you.

A Walk Between
the Sun and Stars

There are some people who become warped under full light.

And it's odd because you'd think you'd be able to see them more full and clear – see every detail and every feature that you'd know for sure it was them – but no. They don't look like the same human being at all.

They are in-fact more themselves when they live and move between the light and shadows.

shihori obata

There's Something in the Walls

I'm not sure if I want to stay here.
Or leave.
There's something in the walls and I don't know what it
does to me.

Perspective

Sometimes it feels as if there's a great distance between you and everything else: Like you're stuck—in some strange time and place where everything feels so wrong. These mere steps between us feel like oceans—yet your heavy heart feels like my own.

It Drizzles

I miss words. Constantly. I often feel incapable of it all: As if I've lost all heart behind this screen of me. And then other times, it all streams out like water and the words pelt down like rain and I look up – and even though I should be relieved – I begin to miss it...

So much more.

How Are You?

I am full of sleepless nights and too often I hear these incoherent murmurs and lullabies. If I could let this feeling live on, I would grow up a child of the moon and sink my feet in running rivers made of stars. If only you could see that. If only you wanted – to be here – with the feelings that are me.

Anger Grows
When We're Not Allowed
To Cry

When Time Blurs

There are moments in time when I'll stop and let the feeling overcome me – Catch up to me – that there is someone there – Someone that should be there – Yet isn't really all there. It's as if I know, that moment in time isn't for me – or for anyone nor anything nor nothing of this world. There is someone else there – that this moment is looking for.

We Don't See Each Other

The sea drowns in the sand –
To no end.
The things that fall –
I won't be able to see again.
Because the more I scrape the earth below,
The more the hole inside me grows.

Please Introduce
The Universe to Me

There are things between the mind and I
A hundred shadows.
And the vague image of people,
Faces.

I still don't know who I am.
I see me between worlds – in conversations amidst ghosts
and unborn anomalies.
There are a hundred lives that live –

Far inside – The deeper me.

Where do All My Feelings Go?

I want to not know...
As absurd as that sounds.
I want to be lost forever
Despite being so afraid.

I often wonder
Would this all be too much in the end?

I like living in this faded world
And getting lost
In the eyes of people
Because I've found that that's where all the colors live –

Far inside the eyes.

There are two moons between us.
And two oceans to cross.

A Town that Disappeared

I'm afraid I don't remember. There is a place that has disappeared here and in this empty place lives sad souls reliving memories that end here.

29

Alike

I couldn't see the difference
And I had left the idea of you behind
— And sometimes I still feel it.
Wandering through a maze of corridors
And chasing the same doors I chase.

But I Still Can't Find You

The last thing I remember.
Is something I can't see.
Something stitched to reality.

Shadows sitting under trees.
A lonely corner of a room.
Emptiness and silence –

And then – you moved.

I think you became something else –
In my poetry.

A Letter
To a Younger Me

Our past fades to a place as far as the stars.
Find solace in the night skies.

Please – Don't be scared anymore.

Things that Come Out at Night

There are things inside me that come out at night. And in my dreams, I find myself with memories I don't have and years I have not lived and I know no longer the idea of people.

Dream Walker

There is another entire world in darkness. People live in it. They breathe it in and out. Their eyes are the stars and their thoughts, the wisps of the cosmos.

They tell me I'm living in a wrong world. I cross things from one place to another that shouldn't belong — But I need to. The place I make waits for me.

Stepping into Stardust

There are a thousand other stars that swim beneath and I still couldn't get the idea out of me – that I wanted something more than just galaxies.

Before I Forget You

She came to me in a dream, as distant as stars beneath closed eyes – And she left just as fast between blinks. And the longing – it swept over me like a wave – too late – a silence with words she wanted to say. And I'm afraid she's lost forever in a place and in a state between dreams and some – other lonely place.

Things I Didn't Know
Until I Met You

Sometimes you'll find
That there is a ghost
That lives there –
In your mind.

Wallflower

I couldn't understand what this space was for – so I've always kept it empty –

For you.

Eyes and Lullabies

Your eyes always saw more than I could see and it made me look inside – looking for my own eyes.

shihori obata

Do You See Them Too?

The night hides gentle creatures and oftentimes they're the only ones who stay.

41

Today

There is always a time – every now and then – when the feelings don't stay in anymore.

And it comes out – as something else.

My Love

Could you tell me one more time – the rain is coming down upon us as constant as the thrum of gray. Invisible. And my eye lids keep falling to the sound of it all – your voice – the world and the night's white noise.

Akai Ito

I think there's a thread in me
That runs to you.
Because my heart gets torn
For no reason –
But your's.

I Think
We Think Alike

How could I have known?

To shift eyes and stumble on steps. To think my thoughts against the wind and skip ahead from this place to the next – and even then, go farther on. I hardly have any other place to belong than here. But still... How could I have known of a place called there – where you and I, my dear, will one day pass as mere strangers.

And fall.

The Things I Haven't Touched

Maybe... this whole time – I wasn't looking for happiness at all. Because in my search for it, I drew farther and farther than I ever could from the root of my own sadness. The whole time, all I wished – was to be truly me. And that meant facing a very dangerous and completely different sort of loneliness and rejection like nothing else in this world.

Words That
Never Finish

"I shouldn't have done that. Letting us part the way we did."

I tore my hand a mere inch away – testing something. Time – I suppose. But something between us broke away and it was all too late for me to catch the pieces that crashed away – to dust. And your gaze fell away.

I didn't do it right...Even now.

Outcast of the Night

There is a time during the night when the stars disappear here. And an eerie feeling settles among us – As if we've been left all to ourselves in a darkness that sinks deeper than sleep.

Slightly Inclined

The more people I have around me, the more alone I feel. From –
this far away – I look at you and wonder if perhaps, by any far off
chance, you feel the same way I do.

Flawless Sorrow

Take your time to see through – to another side. Desperately, I fell for things that weren't there and love that never grew – between... Because, the stars were never there and there were clouds that never left these eyes of mine. Rain and storms – they come and go. And I doubt I'll ever be rid of this pain – being me.

Lonely Belonging

I know I don't belong there anymore.
But I can't help but wonder – When I return – How would it feel?
I can sort of imagine not feeling anything at all – As if I had never
left. Because – Even now, when I am this far away, I can feel a
remnant of myself still living there. A place as voided to me as the
past.

Yet –
I can't go back.

I Want to Know You

There are marks in this corner
I've never made –
In a corner –
In a place –

Of a universe
Where there is only me
Who exists.

An Unconventional
Heart

Some relationships are like two mirrors looking into
one another.

It Takes Time
To Grow

The place I live – is far away.
The feelings that reach you – don't reach me. But that's
okay – because I know even the heart will grow from
nothing.

A Place in Reality

There are moments in time
That split.

And our minds, confused, mend that break in space as if –
it was a dream.

Between Our Eyes that Fall

And the World is Beautiful
Again.

Lovely Eyes

I don't blame you.
I don't blame anyone in-fact.

My heart would rather be nice to you –
More than being nice to me.

Lost in Touch

You were terrified – of time in façade and normalcy. And I should have been there to touch you – to not be able to reach you. Because nothing I said could be heard in there. You were disappearing – and nothing I did could keep you here with me.

You became a ghost to me.

World in Paradox

It is love – yet it hurts so much.

It hurts to get close, but it hurts even more to leave it behind.

We Still Talk

Maybe when we pass –
We will walk with the living in their dreams
And see a world they couldn't share with us in words
Only in trance
And memory.

Love and Fear

I left you
In a place where I was wrong
And you saw sides of me
That didn't care
When all I wanted to do was
Change every part of me that
Fell.

That Is Why...

He had become so used to people not believing him that his identity slowly became everything he couldn't ever be.

Reminiscent

It took everything I had and loved — And replaced it with just one
thing.

I Miss You Again

There was no one there – but the wind and it brought to me your eyes. Twenty-one days have passed and the clear blue sky still echoes your laugh. And for a moment, when the wind reaches to touch my hand, I finally get to see you – again.

You Who Are
Too Much to Me

I know you're just one entity. One human being. But your presence fills the world and you don't go on...

You stain everything.

In Series

I still don't know what place my mind is trying to find its way back to.

I Couldn't Speak the Words
The Way they Came to Me

Black Ink

There is rain forever pouring in my mind. A black water, thick as ink, rising up my soul. And when I think I can handle no more, that's when it finally lets me go.

Beneath the Awning and Forest's Shade

Spring's breath
Clinging to a warm finger
The butterfly shivers.

Dead Language

I listen to the sounds of things I don't understand.
And learn an innate language that doesn't exist outside.
The closest I get to comprehension is in my dreams – but even then,
the mind still stays confused.
Bewildered to languages inside ourselves
That become lost
Like everything else
In translation.

A Human Condition

I was the kind of person who wouldn't ask for help
Even when I was dying.

I Came to Know
A Kinder World

Their words were sad.

Words you hear from them are hardly truths. They are spoken to create this other human being – not them. Listen – instead – to their silence. And pay attention to their gestures, actions – their eyes and intentions. They are worlds better – more good – than what all their own words can relay.

I'm Here Too

There is another person out there – In this dead of the night –
Curled up beneath blankets
With eyes open to darkness
Thinking –
"How am I supposed to do this by myself?"
"How am I to continue living…
by myself?"

I fell, you see, in the beginning – Through dark eyes –
And saw the world at last through another's soul
And the burden became shared.

Through a commonality –
Of two lost souls.
Both saved by each other.

Choose to Love

Do you dream
With someone else?

When empty touches break the skin
And oceans fall from pretty eyes
You can take your sad words
And put them here.

If I cry – it's because my heart
Left to live with you.

Love and Poetry

I'll hide feelings from myself.

And when I've begun to think they've disappeared –
I see it again. In these words.
And my eyes turn soft and I finally begin to listen to myself.

How Long is Forever?

Look at the world long enough and it'll start to fade.

To white.

*****

shihori obata

A special thanks to you
For giving me a chance.

Thank you.

About the Author

Shihori Obata is a Japanese-American poet and painter, born in New Jersey and currently resides in North Carolina. She is a shy, little human just looking for inspiration in the little things. She is constantly on the lookout for pieces and words and colors that keep her heart a-beat...to let her live amongst her poetry.

shihori obata

Website: shihoriobata.com

Instagram: @shihoriobata

Pinterest: pinterest.com/shihoriobata

Etsy Shop: etsy.com/shop/shihoriobata

Tumblr: shihoriobata.tumblr.com

Twitter: @shihoriobata

CPSIA information can be obtained
at www.ICGtesting.com
Printed in the USA
BVOW03s1915231117
501123BV00001B/136/P